CONT

PREFACE

So you and your fiancé(e) agreed to write your own wedding vows and now you are wondering what you were thinking. Maybe you have never been a writer, or you have tried to write in the past and not really impressed anyone. Well, with a little help anyone can write beautiful and memorable wedding vows. What is more, since they are your vows and they come from your heart to the love of your life, there is very little chance of getting them wrong. Of course, you do want to put your best foot forward.

In this brief book we will give you some guidelines and resources that we have shared with hundreds of people that will help you write wedding vows that will make your fiancé(e)'s heart melt like hot butter. In fact, even if you have never been good at poetry, you can sound like Shakespeare with just a little help from the pros. To be perfectly honest, it comes easier for some than for others. Most people do not have the "poetic gene." It will require effort on your part. You cannot wait for some poetic lightning to strike and magically give you the perfect words, but you may be surprised at how the passionate and poetic words will begin to flow from your mind and heart through your fingertips onto the paper with just a little prompting from the suggestions in this book. Then how easily they will flow from you to your wife or husband on your wedding day. In fact, this little book may help you in several areas of your life from romance to work to public speaking. May it be a blessing to you for many years to come.

Dr. Kelly Carr

1. REALLY WANT TO WRITE YOUR OWN VOWS?

Every couple is unique and every wedding ceremony has its own style. For more than 25 years I have attended and performed hundreds of weddings. Each one is singular and diverse. There are no generic people. There are no generic marriage ceremonies. Each person is unique and individual in a thousand different ways and in the same way each wedding ceremony is distinctive. Yet each human being has many similarities and every wedding ceremony has certain basic parts. The following elements are almost always present in a ceremony: the processional, opening remarks, the presentation of the bride, the minister's message or remarks about love and marriage, the wedding vows, the exchanging of rings, the kiss, the presentation of the new couple, and the recessional. Each of these different elements has a number of distinct alternates and variations that can add beauty, personality, and distinctiveness to your most exquisite day.

It is not necessary to write your own unique wedding vows in order to make your wedding unique. Many couples start out on this journey believing that they must write their own original wedding vows. Perhaps some of their married friends wrote their own vows and they were amazed. Maybe the bride or the groom has a romantic or poetic flair and has always dreamed of writing and saying their own self-written vows. Even though it may come easily to them, they do not realize how difficult it may be for others. Or maybe they saw a romantic comedy in which the main characters wrote their own vows and they sounded so beautiful and romantic and everything turned out perfect in the end. Keep in mind that they were actors and they had professional writers. Nevertheless, writing your own vows is nice, but not necessary.

There are also so many elements that may be combined to make the wedding ceremony personal. Music is something that brings such a sense of wonder. It creates atmosphere and reveals the backgrounds and personalities of the couple and their friends and family. I have heard classical, pop, country, jazz, rock, gospel, contemporary Christian music (and the beat goes on) woven beautifully into the many elements of the service. Use the music of your heart and your heritage. Special singers or instrumentals can be included after the presentation of the bride, after the giving of the rings, during the candle or sand ceremony and almost any place you wish.

In addition, there are several symbolic ceremonies that can be included in the service. The Unity Candle and the Sand Ceremony both symbolize the union of the husband and wife in a wonderful and inseparable way. Since they symbolize the same thing, it is best to choose one or the other. Candles are always risky if your wedding venue is outside because of the wind.

Other things that make a wedding unique are the venue, the wedding dress, the bridesmaids dresses, the decorations, the wedding cake, the reception, the centerpieces, the DJ, and the list goes on. Having said all of this, the point is that you should not feel that your wedding will not be unique unless you write out your own wedding vows. The point here is not to talk you out of writing your wedding vows, you would not have purchased the book if you did not have a real interest in creating them, but if the motive is simply because you feel that is the only way to have an original ceremony, then be at ease.

.

2. TEN TIPS FOR WRITING MEMORABLE VOWS

You can write wedding vows that will make your fiancé(e)'s heart dance for joy, even if you have never been good at poetry. With a little help from the pros, you will be shining like Shakespeare. OK, it comes easier for some than for others. Unless you have the creative or poetic gene, it will require effort. But you will be surprised at how it will come to you with just a little prompting from the list below.

Let me quickly add that writing your own vows is not essential to make your ceremony special. It is special because you are there. The bride and groom, two unique people with different backgrounds, personalities, families, even hopes and dreams, who have been mysteriously and providentially drawn together with a deep love and are willing to devote themselves to each other exclusively for life. Do not feel as though writing your own vows is necessary to making your wedding ceremony original. However, if it is your conviction or desire to do so, then following some of these simple principles listed below, you will be able to write some very elegant vows that will express your true love and commitment, delight your fiancé(e), amaze your guests, and may even surprise you.

Below you will find ten tips for writing beautiful, original, personalized vows. There is a brief line or quote after each tip which is intended to be an example to get your creative juices flowing. Perhaps the example will just nudge your memory into action. Explore all of these. However, do not feel compelled to use all ten. Only use the principles which apply most to you.

While you do not need to use all ten tips, however, you do need to use #10. Remember that these are your wedding vows. You are not just promising to be best friends for life; lots of people who never get married do that. You are pledging to live together as husband and wife. It is a legally binding vow. Do not forget to state that. Be sure to let the minister read through your vows ahead of time and ask if he or she has any suggestions. It would also be a good idea to have someone who is good with grammar to proofread them for you and offer suggestions. While you may want your vows to be a surprise to your fiancé(e), you do not want to embarrass yourself by reading bad grammar in front of a crowd.

Two suggestions to think about as you work through each of these tips below. First, ask yourself, "how did / does that make me feel?" Second, ask yourself, "what did / does it make me want to do?" E.g. "You looked so beautiful the first day I saw you (how did I feel?) that I just had to meet you, and (what did I want to do?) I knew I would do whatever it took to be near you forever."

#1 Think about how and where you met.

"When we first met I was captivated by your ... and now I am even more..."

"The first time I saw you, you were helping a group of ...I knew at that moment that I wanted to spend the rest of my life with you."

"Aruba is the most beautiful place on earth, and when we met there it was like a dream come true, but its beauty faded in comparison to yours that day..."

"The day we met it seemed like an accident, but the more I have thought about it, that day was planned in eternity."

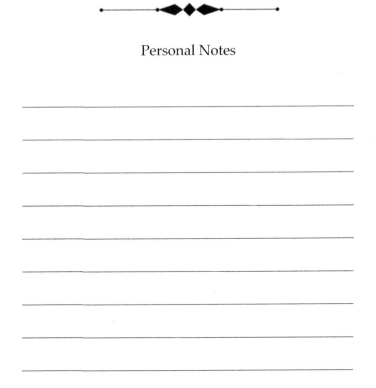

Personal Notes

_____

_____

_____

_____

_____

_____

_____

_____

_____

#2 Highlight your love's most excellent qualities.

"I love you for..." or "I admire the way..."

Here are a few suggestions: sense of humor, patience, acceptance, enthusiasm for life, goodness, the way you see the good in me...

Personal Notes

#3 Recall what you have enjoyed doing together so far.

"The time we spent rafting down the Grand Canyon were the most exciting days of my life, and I know that with you there will be many more of them."

"Going to…with you was my soul's delight"

•●●●•

Personal Notes

_____

_____

_____

_____

_____

_____

_____

_____

_____

_____

_____

_____

_____

#4 Think of trials you have endured together.

"I would never have been able to ... without your tender encouragement. And I know we will be able to weather any storm that may come in the future."

"When I went through...I thought I would never be able to get through it, but having you by my side, made all the difference."

Personal Notes

_____

_____

_____

_____

_____

_____

_____

_____

_____

_____

_____

#5 Thank God for bringing them into your life.

"I am so grateful to God for bringing you into my life..."

"I could never thank God enough for bringing us together."

———◆◆———

Personal Notes

_____

_____

_____

_____

_____

_____

_____

_____

_____

_____

_____

_____

_____

_____

#6 **Remember the person you have always dreamed of marrying.**

"I always dreamed of marrying someone strong and handsome, but you are so much more than I dreamed."

"When I used to dream of having a wife and a family, I hoped I would be with someone pretty, but I had no idea that God would send me an angel."

Personal Notes

_____

_____

_____

_____

_____

_____

_____

_____

_____

_____

_____

_____

#7 Imagine what life will be like together.

"I look forward to coming home to your tender and loving arms every day. I look forward to sharing our joys and even our trials together."

"When I think about the future, I cannot imagine not seeing you every day. I cannot imagine a future without your smile, your laugh, your touch..."

—————•●●•—————

Personal Notes

_____

_____

_____

_____

_____

_____

_____

_____

_____

_____

_____

#8 Refer to the various roles you will be playing in your marriage.

"I am eager to be your helper, confidant, encourager, lover, and friend."

"What a privilege and a joy it will be to be the one you go to when you are afraid, when you are discouraged, when you want to share a laugh, when you see a bug..."

(You can also refer to the sample vows for some of these ideas.)

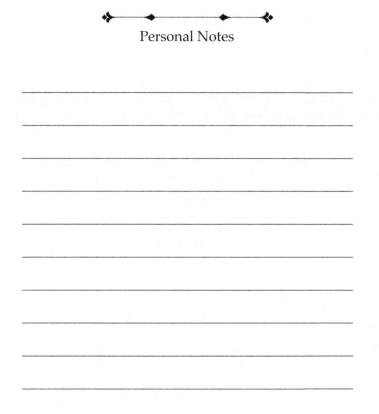

Personal Notes

#9 Enlist the help of the greatest poets, Bible verses, and love songs of all time.

(See the list of "Fifty Quotes of Love" and "Fifty Quotes of Marriage" in chapter 5 and chapter 6.)

"A wise man once said of marriage, 'Never above you. Never below you. Always beside you.' That is what I believe builds a strong marriage, and I pledge to never strive to be over you or never sink beneath you, but to always stand strong and faithfully at your side as we face the adventure of life together."

"The Bible says that 'love never fails.' Because I know that my love for you is from God, I know it will never fail. Please take this ring as a symbol of my love and as a seal of our marriage."

Someone said that a friend's love says, " If you ever need anything, I'll be there." But my love for you says: "You'll never need anything; I'll always be there."

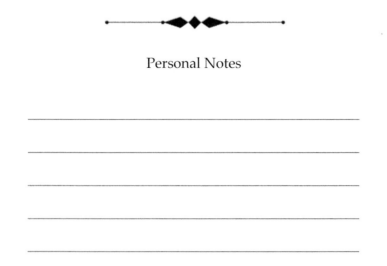

Personal Notes

_____

_____

_____

_____

_____

#10 Vow to be a faithful husband or wife.

Remember that this is the marriage vow. It is more than a poem, or a personal statement. It is a legally binding vow of marriage. You must say that you promise to be a faithful or devoted husband or wife. *"I give myself to you as your husband / wife for as long as life shall last."*

----------◆----------

Personal Notes

_____

_____

_____

_____

_____

_____

_____

_____

_____

_____

_____

_____

_____

One final tip. Keep your vows under 3 minutes. There will be other elements in your wedding ceremony that will take time. Most people are really good at speaking in front of a crowd for 1 or 2 minutes. Your vows do not have to be poetic to be effective. The most important thing is that they state your true feelings of love and commitment, with sincerity and your own personality. (Just to be on the safe side, give a printed copy of your vows to the minister to carry in his coat pocket in case you misplace your copy.)

Use the following pages to make a few notes to help you get started.

Personal Notes

_____

_____

_____

_____

_____

_____

_____

_____

_____

_____

Personal Notes

_____

_____

_____

_____

_____

_____

_____

_____

_____

_____

_____

_____

_____

_____

_____

_____

_____

3. WEDDING VOWS OR A PERSONAL STATEMENT?

As was stated earlier, it is not necessary to write your own wedding vows in order for your wedding ceremony to be original. Some couples opt for a personal statement in place of personalized vows. Many ceremonies contain special readings. There are many popular readings such as "The Art of Marriage" or 1 Corinthians chapter 13. These verses and others are read because they resonate with the bride and groom. A personal statement written by the bride and groom is similar to including a special reading in the ceremony.

One trend I have noticed in recent years, in place of a couple writing their own wedding vows or ring vows, is to write a personal statement instead. It is much the same thing as writing customized wedding vows, however, it leaves out the vow to be husband or wife. It states the love, the feeling, the emotion, the happiness of the relationship and the occasion without actually having to add in the words that actually vow to legally become husband and wife. So the same basic formula as described in chapter 2 may be used to write a personal statement.

Using a personal statement instead of personalized wedding vows also has the benefit of retaining the richness of the traditional wedding vows. Many couples and parents and friends would consider it a tragedy to not hear the wedding vows that were similar to the vows they made to one another on their own wedding day. Making a personal statement gives the best of both worlds. Another benefit is that since it is slightly less formal and official than the actual wedding vows, there is less pressure on the bride or groom to be "word perfect" in the memorization and recitation of the vows or even in the reading of those vows.

If the couple were to opt for a personal statement in place of writing their own wedding vows, then the ceremony would go something like this. After the welcome, presentation of the bride, message or homily by the minister, and just before beginning the wedding vows, the minister would say, "At this time, Jack and Jill have something special they would like to say to each other..." Or, "Before we proceed with the wedding vows, Jack and Jill both have a brief personal statement they would like to read." Then the minister would turn to the groom and say, "Jack, what would you like to say to your beautiful bride on this your wedding day?" After the groom is finished, the minister would then turn to the bride and say, "And Jill, what would you like to say to your loving husband on this your wedding day?"

After both the bride and groom have had the opportunity to say or read their own statements, then the minister will say, "Jack and Jill, having understood what marriage is and having stated your love and devotion to one another, if you know of no barrier to this union, will you join your right hands together?" The minister will then proceed with the wedding vows beginning with the groom's vows and then the bride's vows. It is very simple to incorporate this brief statement into the wedding ceremony and generally takes less than five minutes unless you have a particularly long winded person. So be sure you time yourself reading your statement before your wedding and keep it under three minutes each.

.

4. CLASSIC WEDDING VOWS AND RING VOWS

When people discuss wedding vows or ask for a copy of the wedding vows, they often do not realize that there are many kinds of vows that come from the many different traditions. Here we discuss Christian wedding vows that come from the different traditions or denominations.

It is also important to note that in most Christian wedding ceremonies, there are actually two sets of vows: the "wedding vows," to which the bride or the groom simply has to answer "I do" or "I will," and the "ring vows," which are usually "repeat-after-me" vows.

Most couples that I have worked with who want to write their own vows are really referring to the "wedding vows" and not the "ring vows."

These classic wedding vows and ring vows are included here as a reference for couples who wish to write their own vows. Reading through them may help them see what the vows really mean and clarify some thoughts on how to word their own vows.

Traditional Christian "Wedding Vows"

(to the Groom) Do you [Name], in the presence of God and these assembled witnesses, promise to love and to cherish, in sickness and in health, in prosperity and in adversity, this woman whose right hand you now hold? Do you promise to be to her in all things a true and faithful husband, to be devoted unto her, and to her only, as long as life shall last? And do you take her to be your lawful, wedded wife, as long as you both shall live? Do you? (He answers "I do.")

(to the Bride) Do you, [Name], in the presence of God and these assembled witnesses, promise to love and to cherish, in sickness and in health, in prosperity and in adversity, this young man whose right hand you now hold? Do you promise to be to him in all things a true and faithful wife, to be devoted unto him, and to him only, as long as life shall last? Do you take him to be your lawfully, wedded husband, as long as you both shall live? Do you? (She answers, "I do.")

Episcopalian Wedding Vows

"In the Name of God, I [Name], take you, [Name], to be my [husband/wife], to have and to hold from this day forward, for better, for worse, for richer, for poorer, in sickness and in health, to love and to cherish, until we are parted by death. This is my solemn vow."

Presbyterian Wedding Vows

"I, [Name], take you to be my wedded [husband/wife], and I do promise and covenant, before God and these witnesses, to be your loving and faithful [husband/wife], in plenty and in want, in joy and in sorrow, in sickness and in health, as long as we both shall live."

Methodist Wedding Vows

"In the Name of God, I [Name], take you, [Name], to be my [husband/wife], to have and to hold from this day forward, for better, for worse, for richer, for poorer, in sickness and in health, to love and to cherish, until we are parted by death. This is my solemn vow."

Baptist Wedding Vows

"I, [Name], take thee, [Name], to be my wedded [husband/wife], to have and to hold, from this day forward, for better for worse, for richer, for poorer, in sickness and in health, to love and to cherish, till death do us part, according to God's holy ordinance; and thereto I pledge thee my faith."

Catholic Wedding Vows

I, [Name], take thee, [Name], for my lawful wife / husband, to have and to hold, from this day forward, for better for worse, for richer for poorer, in sickness and health, until death do us part.

Also

I, [Name], take you, [Name], to be my husband / wife, I promise to be true to you in good times and in bad, in sickness and in health. I will love you and honor you all the days of my life.

Lutheran Wedding Vows

I take you, [Name], to be my husband / wife, from this day forward, to join with you and share all that is to come, and I promise to be faithful to you until death parts us.

Also

Will you have this woman / man, to be your wedded wife / husband, to live together in holy matrimony? Will you love her / him, comfort her / him, honor and keep her / him in sickness and in health, in sorrow and in joy, and, forsaking all others, be faithful to her / him as long as you both shall live?

Answer: I do, or I will

Funny Wedding Vows

"Wilt thou take this woman to be your wedded wife, to live together in holy matrimony? Wilt though love her, comfort her, honor and keep her, in sickness and health, in sorrow and joy? Wilt thou forsake all others and support her as long as you both shall live?

He said, "I wilt." And he did.

Traditional Christian "Ring Vows"

Minister's Part

"What token do you have today to give to your Bride/Husband as a symbol of your love and as a seal of your marriage?" (Answer = "A Ring")

(Best Man or Ring Bearer or Maid of Honor steps forward and presents the ring to the Bride / Groom.)

Or

"Now may I have a token of your sincerity that you will keep these vows?"
(The Best Man or Ring Bearer or Maid of Honor steps forward and presents the ring to the Minister.)

Comments about the significance of the rings.

The ring vows below are only shown once, however, the groom repeats them after the minister when he places the ring on his bride's finger. The bride also repeats them after the minister when she places the ring on her husband's finger. Usually, the names are used, e.g. "I [John Doe], give you, [Jane Smith],"etc. Also, the minister needs to use short phrases since these are usually "repeat-after-me" vows.

Protestant Ring Vows

I give you this ring as a symbol of my love; and with all that I am and all that I have, I honor you, in the name of the Father, and of the Son, and of the Holy Spirit.

Episcopalian Ring Vows

[Name/Groom/Bride], I give you this ring as a symbol of my vow, and with all that I am and all that I have, I honor you, in the name of the Father, and of the Son, and of the Holy Spirit.

Presbyterian Ring Vows

This ring I give you, in token and pledge of our constant faith and abiding love.

Roman Catholic Ring Vows

In the name of the Father, the Son, and the Holy Spirit, take and wear this ring as sign of my love and faithfulness.

Lutheran Ring Vows

I give you this ring as a sign of my love and faithfulness. Receive this ring as a token of wedded love and faith.

Methodist Ring Vows

[Name/Groom/Bride], I give you this ring as a sign of my vow, and with all that I am, and all that I have; I honor you in the name of the Father, and of the Son, and of the Holy Spirit. Amen.

Baptist Ring Vows

With this ring I thee wed, and all my worldly goods I thee endow. In sickness and in health, in poverty or in wealth, till death do us part..

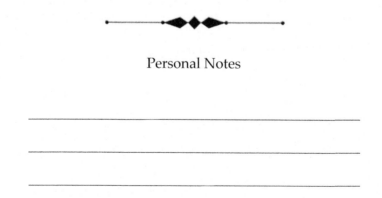

Personal Notes

_____

_____

_____

Personal Notes

_____

_____

_____

_____

_____

_____

_____

_____

_____

_____

_____

_____

_____

_____

_____

_____

_____

_____

_____

_____

5. FIFTY QUOTES OF LOVE

Love is so very special
Yet can make you feel so lost
It can arrive just like the springtime
And melt away like morning frost

You must find ways to nurture
Always grow your love with care
Never ever take for granted
The love that you both share

Mistakes are bound to happen
You may hurt each other's heart
Yet don't give up to easily
It will tear your love apart

Love resembles a bright flame
That lights a dark starry night
Never ever let this flame burn down
Rekindle with all your might

Take a moment every day
Look deep into each other's eyes
Never hesitate to show affection
Small gestures will keep a love alive

Talk openly about your feelings
Take time to show that you care
Treasure each and every moment
Because to find true love is rare
Connie Thomas Lugo

Love has nothing to do with what you are expecting to get...
Only with what you are expected to give. . . .
Which is everything.
Katharine Hepburn

Love is like playing the piano.
First you must learn to play by the rules,
then you must forget the rules
and play from your heart.
Unknown

The Magic Of Love

Love is like magic
And it always will be.
For love still remains
Life's sweet mystery!!
Love works in ways
That are wondrous and strange

And there's nothing in life
That love cannot change!!
Love can transform
The most commonplace
Into beauty and splendor
And sweetness and grace.
Love is unselfish,
Understanding and kind,
For it sees with its heart
And not with its mind!!
Love is the answer
That everyone seeks...
Love is the language,
That every heart speaks.
Love can't be bought,
It is priceless and free,
Love, like pure magic,
Is life's sweet mystery!!
- Helen Steiner Rice –

Love is not about finding the right person,
but creating a right relationship.
It's not about how much love you have in the beginning
but how much love you build till the end.
Author Unknown

LOVE: The irresistible desire to be irresistibly desired.
Mark Twain

What's love?

Love is...
What makes a weak man brave
And a king step off his throne
Good times, bad times
Easy times, tough times
It comes in an instant
And lasts three days after forever
That's what love is.
- Mike –

A Friend's Love says:
" If you ever need anything, I'll be there."

True Love says:
" You'll never need anything; I'll be there."
Jimi Hollemans

Love, like a river, will cut a new path
whenever it meets an obstacle.
Crystal Middlemas

A funny thing is love. It cometh from above,
and lighteth like a dove—on some.
And some whom it hits, it nearly gives them fits,
and scatters all their wits—Oh hum!

Love: The last word in a letter or telegram.

I am my beloved's and my beloved is mine.
Song of Solomon 6:3

"Love covereth a multitude of sins."
1 Peter 4:8

In jealousy there is more of self-love, than of love to another.
LaRochefoucauld

The course of true love never did run smooth.
Shakespeare

No man at one time can be wise and love.
Robert Herrick

Then, must you speak of one that loved not wisely but too
well; of one not easily jealous, but being wrong perplex'd in
the extreme.
Shakespeare

33

There's beggary in the love that can be reckon'd.
Shakespeare

Tis better to have loved and lost
than never to have loved at all.
Tennyson

In charity (love) there is no excess.
Francis Bacon

Love does not consist in gazing at each other
but in looking together in the same direction.
Antoine De Saint-Exupery

Man's love is of man's life a part;
it is woman's whole existence.
Byron

There is nothing half so sweet in life as love's young dream.
T. Moore

It is astonishing how little one feels poverty when he loves.
Bulwer

Love is an ocean of emotions,
entirely surrounded by expenses.
Lord Dewar

Faults are thick where love is thin.

You will find as you look back upon your life that the
moments when you have really lived are the moments when
you have done things in the spirit of love.
Henry Drummond

Many waters cannot quench love,
neither can the floods drown it.
Song of Solomon 8:7

The course of love never did run smooth.
Shakespeare

Greater love hath no man than this,
that a man lay down his life for his friends.
Jesus (John 15:13)

The most important thing a father can do for his children is
to love their mother.
Theodore M. Hesburgh

If there is anything better than being loved, it's loving.

My True Love Hath My Heart

My true love hath my heart, and I have his,
By just exchange one for another given;
I hold his dear, and mine he cannot miss,
There never was a better bargain driven;
My true love hath my heart, and I have his.

His heart in me keeps him and mine in one,
My heart in him his thoughts and senses guides:
He loves my heart, for once it was his own,
I cherish his because in me it hides:
My true love hath my heart, and I have his.
Sir John Philip Sidney

Eskimo Love Song

You are my [husband / wife]
My feet shall run because of you.
My feet, dance because of you.
My heart shall beat because of you.
My eyes, see because of you.
My mind, think because of you.
And I shall love because of you.

Sonnet XVIII

Shall I compare thee to a summer's day?
Thou art more lovely and more temperate.
Rough winds do shake the darling buds of May,
And summer's lease hath all too short a date:
Sometimes too hot the eye of heaven shines,
And often is his gold complexion dimmed:
And every fair from fair sometimes declines,
By chance or nature's changing course, untrimmed:
But thy eternal summer shall not fade
Nor lose possession of that fair thou owest;
Nor shall Death brag thou wonderest in his shade
When in eternal lines to time thou growest.
So long as men can breathe or eyes can see
So long lives this, and this gives life to thee.
Shakespeare

Love at first sight is nothing special. It's when two people
have been looking at each other for years
that it becomes a miracle.
Sam Levinson

Sonnet CXVI

Let me not to the marriage of true minds
Admit impediments. Love is not love
Which alters when it alteration finds,
Or bends with the remover to remove.
O no! It is an ever-fixed mark
That looks on tempests, and is never shaken:
It is the star to every wandering bark,
Whose worth's unknown, although his height be taken.
Love's not Time's fool, though rosy lips and cheeks
Within his bending sickle's compass come;
Love alters not with his brief hours and weeks,
But bears it out even to the edge of doom.
If this be error and upon me proved,
I never writ, nor no man ever loved.
Shakespeare

A Thing of Beauty
From Endymion

A thing of beauty is a joy for ever:
It's loveliness increases; it will never
Pass into nothingness, but still will keep
A bower quiet for us, and a sleep
Full of sweet dreams, and health, and quiet breathing,
John Keats

A Red, Red Rose

O my Luve's like a red, red rose
That's newly sprung in June:
O my Luve's like the melodie
That's sweetly play'd in tune!

As fair art thou, my bonnie lass,
So deep in luve am I:
And I will luve thee still, my dear,
Till a' the seas gang dry:

Till a" the seas gang dry, my dear,
And the rocks melt wi' the sun;
I will luve thee still, my dear,
While the sands o' life shall run.

And fare thee weel, my only Luve,
And fare thee weel a while!
And I will come again, my Luve,
Tho' it were ten thousand mile.
Robert Burns

May the Lord make your love increase and overflow.
1 Thessalonians 3:12

A friend loves at all times.
Proverbs 17:17

Love's Philosophy

The fountains mingle with the river,
And the rivers with the ocean,
The winds of heaven mix forever
With a sweet emotion;
Nothing in the world is single;
All things by a law divine
In one another's being mingle;
Why not I with thine?

See the mountains kiss high heaven,
And the waves clasp one another;
No sister flower would be forgiven
If it disdained it brother;
And the sunlight clasps the earth,
And the moonbeams kiss the sea;
What are all these kissings worth,
If thou kiss not me?
Percy Bysshe Shelley

The best and most beautiful things in the world cannot be
seen or even touched. They must be felt with the heart.
Helen Keller

This ring is round and hath no end;
so is my love unto my friend.

Why Do I Love You?

I love you,
Not only for what you are,
But for what I am
When I am with you.

I love you
Not only for what
You have made of yourself,
But for what
You are making of me.

I love you
For ignoring the possibilities
Of the fool in me
And for laying firm hold
Of the possibilities for good.

Why do I love you?

I love you
For closing your eyes
To the discords--
And for adding to the music in me
By worshipful listening.

I love you because you
Are helping me to make
Of the lumber of my life
Not a tavern
But a temple;
And out of the words

Of my every day
Not a reproach
But a song.

I love you
Because you have done
More than any creed
To make me happy.

You have done it
Without a word,
Without a touch,
Without a sign.
You have done it
Just by being yourself.

After all
Perhaps that is what
Love means .
Roy Croft

Who can find a virtuous woman?
For her price is far above rubies.
Proverbs 31:10

Set me as a seal upon thine heart, as a seal upon thine arm;
for love is strong as death..."
Song of Solomon 8:6

He brought me to the banqueting house,
and his banner over me was love.
Song of Solomon 2:4

As the apple tree among the trees of the wood, so is my
beloved among the sons.
I sat down under his shadow with great delight,
and his fruit was sweet to my taste.
Song of Solomon 2:3

Thou has turned for me my mourning into dancing;
thou has put off my sackcloth, and girded me with gladness.
Psalm 30:11

Keep me as the apple of the eye;
hide me under the shadow of thy wings.
Psalm 17:8

God is love; and he that dwelleth in love dwelleth in God,
and God in him.
1 John 4:16

6. FIFTY QUOTES OF MARRIAGE

Marriage is not a ritual or an end.
It is a long, intricate,
intimate dance together
and nothing matters more
than your own sense of balance
and your choice of partner.

You do not marry someone you can live with –
you marry the person who you cannot live without.

Marriage: A period when you make progress if you break
even.
The most dangerous year in married life is the first:
then comes the second, third, fourth, fifth, etc.

Marriage: Has three states—cooing—wedding—billing.

Amy Bloom
One look
One smile
One touch
One embrace
One kiss
One love
Two people
Two minds
Two souls
Two destinies
One road
One journey
One ending
Together.

- Melissa Higgins –

My most brilliant achievement was my ability to be able
to persuade my wife to marry me.
Winston Churchill

Two are better than one,
because they have good return for their work:
If one falls down, his friend can help him up.
But pity the man who falls and has no one to help him up.
Ecclesiastes 4:9-10

Even marriages made in heaven need down to earth
maintenance work.
Lloyd Byers

To keep the fire burning brightly, keep the two logs
together, near enough to keep each other warm, and far
enough apart—about a finger's breadth—for breathing
room. Good fire, good marriage—same rule.
Marnie Reed Crowell

God is the only third party in a marriage
that can make it work.

The key to a perfect marriage is not expecting perfection.

Marriage is an empty box.
It remains empty unless you put in more than you take out.

To keep your marriage brimming,
With love in the loving cup,
When you're wrong, admit it.
When you're right, shut up.
Ogden Nash

Successful marriage is always a triangle:
a man, a woman, and God.
Cecil Myers

There is no more lovely, friendly and charming relationship,
communion or company than a good marriage.
Martin Luther

The harder you work at a relationship,
the harder it is to surrender.

Whoso findeth a wife findeth a good thing.
Proverbs 18:22

A successful marriage requires falling in love many times,
always with the same person.
Mignon McLaughlin

When two fond hearts
As one unite,
The load is easy
And the burden light.

We cannot tell the precise moment when friendship is formed. As in filling a vessel drop by drop there is at last a drop which makes it run over, so in a series of kindnesses there is at last one which makes the heart run over.
Samuel Johnson

Don't walk in front of me,
I may not follow.
Don't walk behind me,
I may not lead.
Walk beside me
And just be my friend.
Albert Camus

I know I've never told you
In the hurried rush of days
How much your friendship helps me
In a thousand little ways;
But you've played such a part
In all I do or try to be,
I want to tell you thank you
For being friends with me.
Anon

When true friends meet in adverse hour;
'Tis like a sunbeam through a shower.
Sir Walter Scott

Whether you are blessed with soulmates…or with those
who walk with you just a little while, not one of these
friends crosses your path by chance. Each is a messenger
sent by God, to give you the wisdom, companionship,
comfort, or challenge you need for a particular leg of your
spiritual journey.
Traci Mullins

If I do vow a friendship, I'll perform it to the last article.
Shakespeare

Friendship is a chain of gold
Shaped in God's all perfect mold.
Each link a smile, a laugh, a tear,
A grip of the hand, a word of cheer.
Steadfast as the ages roll
Binding closer soul to soul;
No matter how far or heavy the load
Sweet is the journey on friendship's road.
Unknown

A true friend is the greatest of all blessings.
La Rochefoucauld

Each shining light above us
Has its own peculiar grace,
But every light of heaven
Is in my darling's face.
John Hay

Never above you.
Never below you.
Always beside you.
Walter Winchell

Marriage is one long conversation, chequered by disputes…
But in the intervals, almost unconsciously, and with no
desire to shine, the whole material of life is turned over and
over ideas are struck out and shared, the two persons more
and more adapt their notions one to suit the other, and in
process of time, without sound of trumpet, they conduct
each other into new worlds of thought.
Robert Louis Stevenson

Grow old along with me!
The best is yet to be.
The last of life, for which the first was made.
Our times are in His hand
Who saith, A whole I planned,
Youth shows but half,
Trust God, see all, nor be afraid!
Robert Browning

The sacred academy of man's life,
Is holy wedlock in a happy wife.
Francis Quarles

A true friend gives freely, advises justly, assists readily,
adventures boldly, takes all patiently, defends courageously,
and continues a friend unchangeable.
William Penn

True friends don't spend time gazing into each other's eyes.
They may show great tenderness toward each other, but
they face in the same direction—toward common projects,
interests, goals—above all, toward a common Lord.
C. S. Lewis

Friendship is one mind in two bodies.
Mencius

Lord, make me an instrument of Your peace. Where there is
hatred let me sow love; where there is injury, pardon; where
there is doubt, faith; where there is despair, hope; where
there is darkness, light; and where there is sadness, joy.
Saint Francis of Assisi

Just thinking about a friend makes you want to do a happy
dance, because a friend is someone who loves you
in spite of your faults.
Charles M. Schulz

A good marriage is not a contract between two persons but a sacred covenant between three. Too often Christ is never invited to the wedding and finds no room in the home. Why? Is it because we have misrepresented Him and forgotten His joyful outlook on life?
Donald T. Kaufman

That voice that breathed o'er Eden,
That earliest wedding day,
The primal marriage blessing,
It hath not passed away.
John Keble

Let nothing break our bond but Death,
For in the world above
'Tis the breaker Death that soldereth
Our ring of Wedded Love.
Gerald Massey

God help the man who won't marry until he finds the perfect woman, and God help him still more if he finds her.
Benjamin Tillett

God, the best maker of all marriages,
Combine your hearts in one.
Shakespeare

Teacher, tender comrade, wife,
A fellow-farer through life.
Robert Louis Stevenson

Love like ours can never die!
Rudyard Kipling

So ought men to love their wives as their own bodies.
He that loveth his wife loveth himself.
Ephesians 5:28

But at the beginning of creation God 'made them male and female. 'For this reason a man will leave his father and mother and be united to his wife, and the two will become one flesh.' So they are no longer two, but one. Therefore what God has joined together, let man not separate.
Mark 10:6-9 NIV

But from the beginning of creation, God MADE THEM MALE AND FEMALE. FOR THIS REASON A MAN SHALL LEAVE HIS FATHER AND MOTHER, AND THE TWO SHALL BECOME ONE FLESH; so they are no longer two, but one flesh. What therefore God has joined together, let no man separate.
Mark 10:6-9 NASB

Blessed is every one that feareth the LORD; that walketh in his ways. For thou shalt eat the labour of thine hands: happy shalt thou be, and it shall be well with thee. Thy wife shall be as a fruitful vine by the sides of thine house: thy children like olive plants round about thy table. Behold, that thus shall the man be blessed that feareth the LORD.
Psalm 128:1-4

Finally, brethren, whatsoever things are true, whatsoever things are honest, whatsoever things are just, whatsoever things are pure, whatsoever things are lovely, whatsoever things are of good report; if there be any virtue, and if there be any praise, think on these things.
Philippians 4:8

A virtuous wife is a crown to her husband.
Proverbs 12:4

God be merciful to us, and bless us,
and cause his face to shine upon us.
Psalm 67:1

The Bible tells us that God created man. God said that it was not good for man to live alone. So He made for a man that which alone would complete him, a woman. From Adam's side God took a rib and made a person to stand beside him. She was not to be ruled by him or to rule him, but to complete him.

In the Garden, God made a woman, not from man's head to rule over him, and not from his feet to be trodden beneath him, but from his side to be equal to him, and from near his heart to be loved by him, and from under his arm to be cherished and protected by him.

The wedding ring is devoted to the beautiful purpose of symbolizing your covenant and commitment to love each other and to live together for as long as you both shall live. The ring is an unending circle which symbolizes a love between you that shall never cease. The ring's untarnished gold represents the lasting quality of your love, a love that shall never grow old.
Morris Chapman.

7. A LIST OF MOST ROMANTIC WORDS

If you have written your vows, but they just do not seem to really "pop." Perhaps you are missing the right word. It was Mark Twain who said, "The difference between the right word and the almost right word is the difference between lightning and the lightning bug." He had a great way of making his point with wit.

This list of more than 150 words is compiled from some of the most romantic poems and songs of all time. These words are often used in romance novels to demonstrate the spark that exists between two lovers or arouse the passion that already exists in their hearts.

After you have written your vows read through this list of words and see if there are any places where you may want to make some substitutions that will take them to the next level.

Love

Romance

Romantic

Hopelessly

Amaze

Dream

Moonlight

Heart

Feel

Come

Arms

Legs

Face

Eyes

Hair

Gentle

Arouse

Excite

Response

Essence

Elegant

Pleasure

Remember

Handle

Never

Whisper

Kiss

Desire

Bliss

Bloom

Destiny

Fire

Flame

Kindle

Spark

Special

Precious

Unique

Tomorrow

Today

Passion

Touch

Friendship

Madly

Melt

Angel

Soul mate

Heaven

Paradise

True

Genuine

Real

Rose

Flower

Nights

Days

Mornings

Star

Soul

Embrace

Perfection

Red

Pink

Ecstasy

Promise

Rendezvous

Secret

Simple

Lover

Sunset

Tender

Suddenly

Thoughts

Cherish

Honor

Gallant

Give

Undying

Meant

Gaze

Wrapped

Splendor

Splendid

Yes

Inspiration

You

Hold

Entice

Thrill

Free

Bound

Burning

Gift

Gorgeous

Knight

Shining

Armor

All

Listening

Hearing

Sunshine

Dance

Believe

Beyond

Deep

Long

Drift

Sail

Endless

Candlelight

Fairy tale

First

Glow

Bright

Hand

Know

Miss, Missing

Ask

Found

Seek

Knock

Entranced

Innermost

Pledge

Handle

Hold

Together

Open

Mine

Ruby

Smile

Sweet

Sweetheart

Rapture

Garden

Prayers

Marry

Complete

Whole

Happy

Meeting

Lips

Yearn

Fantasy

Imagine

Caress

Forever

Always

Eternally

Magic

Completely

Swept

Fall in love

Handsome

Lovely

Beautiful

Exquisite

Courageous

Strong

Masculine

Manly

8. EXAMPLES OF PERSONALIZED VOWS

In this chapter, we will give a number of examples of both wedding vows and ring vows that have been personalized by couples. Some of these wedding vows and ring vows have been composed by the bride and groom themselves. Others have been amended from the wedding vows I typically use by adding a phrase or changing a phrase here or there to make it more personal and meaningful to them. Sometimes the phrases are the same, but the language has been modernized. In some examples, the couple does not mention being "husband" or "wife" during the wedding vows, but they do make that commitment during the ring vows. In these examples, the names have been changed.

Personalized Wedding Vows

(to the Groom) Do you Mark Clinton, in the presence of these assembled witnesses, promise to love and to cherish, in sickness and in health, in prosperity and in adversity, this woman whose right hand you now hold? Do you promise to be to her in all things a true and faithful husband, to be devoted unto her, and to her only, mind, body and soul? And do you take her to be your lawful, wedded wife, from this day forward? (He answers "I do.")

(to the Bride) Do you, Carmen Smith, in the presence of these assembled witnesses, promise to love and to cherish, in sickness and in health, in prosperity and in adversity, this young man whose right hand you now hold? Do you promise to be to him in all things a true and faithful wife, to be devoted unto him, and to him only, mind, body and soul? Do you take him to be your lawfully, wedded husband, from this day forward? (She answers, "I do.")

From this day on, I choose you, my beloved [Joseph / Elizabeth], to be my (husband/wife). To live with you and laugh with you; to stand by your side, and sleep in your arms; to be joy to your heart, and food for your soul; to bring out the best in you always, and, for you, to be the most that I can. I promise to laugh with you in good times, to struggle with you in bad; to solace you when you are downhearted; to wipe your tears with my hands; to comfort you with my body; to mirror you with my soul; to share with you all my riches and honors; to play with you as much as I can until we grow old; and, still loving each other sweetly and gladly, our lives shall come to an end.

Susanna, We share many commonalities and have lots of similar interests. We both enjoy the simple pleasures that life has to offer and we both want the same things out of life. We are both going in the same direction. But what truly draws me to you are the differences between us. They give our relationship and our life a sense of balance. We each have a unique role in our relationship and we each understand our weaknesses.

You are my rock, my solid ground and each time I look at you, it feels like coming home from a long trip. Your stable nature is one of the many things I'm drawn to, probably because, as you are well aware, I am not. You are calculated and well thought out, you analyze before acting. Most everything you do has a purpose and a plan.

You approach your relationships in the same way. You don't just open up and invite people right in. It takes time to build your trust and earn your devotion and I feel all the more special standing here with you today because of that.

With this choice came the responsibility of raising a child. I love you even more still because of the love and dedication that you show to Nicky. You approach your role as mother to him the way you approach everything else you do, with stability, much thought, and your whole heart.

You are definitely the best of both of us and I feel overjoyed and completely beside myself when I think of the strength of the bond that we share. I believe it's a bond that spans beyond a lifetime.

I want you to know that I accept this job with open arms. I promise you today that I will keep your heart safe and guard it with the same, if not more, care and vigilance than you have for so long.

I love you, Jonathan

"Love does not consist in gazing at each other, but in looking together in the same direction".

Angela, from the moment when we first met, I looked forward to our first date, after which I looked forward to our first kiss, then our first weekend trip together. I remember looking forward to my first opportunity to meet your family and friends, and even more looked forward to the time when I could share you with my family and friends. From the moment that you agreed to marry me, I looked forward to the engagement and the joyous process of planning and preparation, and the wonderful day in which I am to marry you. It is with great anticipation that I look forward to my life with you.

You are my best friend and you are my true love. I am better for having met you and known you for the past year, which has felt like so much more than only one year. I look forward to our future together, as I know that with the love we share, the best is yet to come.

I promise to be always earnest and faithful in our marriage and friendship. I promise to always keep your love sacred and to always keep your love tank full. I know that our love will guide us as we continue looking together in the same direction.

I love you.

Stephen, you were in my dreams long before I even knew there was a you and me. It wasn't long after we met, when I realized that I loved you and wanted to spend the rest of my life with you. You are the love of my life, my best friend, my soul mate. I had heard of "soul mates" before, but I never knew such a person could exist until I met you. When I am with you, I know that I am in the presence of someone who makes my life more complete than I ever dreamed it could be. I want you to know that my world is reassured by you and my heart is so thankful that you're here.

May the bond you and I make today never be broken. May the memories we make tomorrow never be forgotten. May the good times make us laugh and the bad times make us stronger. May our love grow more every day. May we cherish the memories of our individual pasts and create our new life as we go along together.

I take you, Stephen, this day as my husband, and I promise to walk by your side forever, as your friend, your wife, your soul mate. I promise to support your dreams and to be there for you all of our lives. I promise to sleep by your side, to be the joy of your heart, the food to your soul, and the best person I can be for you. I promise to laugh with you when times are good and to suffer with you when they are bad. I promise to wash away your tears with my kisses and to hold you tightly until our days on earth are over. You are the one for me and I am proud to marry you today.

"In God's eyes do you, Carlton, solemnly vow, to take, Priscilla, as your lawful wedded wife, to have and to hold, from this day forward, for better or for worse, for richer or for poorer, in sickness and in health, to love and cherish for all eternity?"
"Do You?" Carlton: "I do"

"In God's eyes do you, Priscilla, solemnly vow, to take, Carlton, as your lawful wedded husband, to have and to hold, from this day forward, for better or for worse, for richer or for poorer, in sickness and in health, to love and cherish for all eternity?"
"Do You?" Priscilla: "I do"

Benson, do you promise to encourage and inspire Angelique, to laugh with her, and to comfort her in times of sorrow and struggle? Do you promise to love her in good times and in bad, when life seems easy and when it seems hard, when your love is simple, and when it is an effort? Do you promise to cherish her, and to always hold her in the highest regard?

Angelique, do you promise to encourage and inspire Benson, to laugh with him, and to comfort him in times of sorrow and struggle? Do you promise to love him in good times and in bad, when life seems easy and when it seems hard, when your love is simple, and when it is an effort? Do you promise to cherish him, and to always hold him in the highest regard?

Donald, do you come before this gathering of friends and family to proclaim your love and devotion for Michelle? Do you promise to affirm her, respect her, and care for her during times of joy and hardship? Do you commit yourself to share your feelings of happiness and sadness? Do you pledge to remain faithful to her and her only as long as life shall last? And do you take her to be your lawful, wedded wife, as long as you both shall live? Do you? ("I Do")

Michelle, do you come before this gathering of friends and family to proclaim your love and devotion for Donald? Do you promise to affirm him, respect him, and care for him during times of both joy and hardship? Do you commit yourself to share your feelings of happiness and sadness? Do you pledge to remain faithful to him and him only as long as life shall last? And do you take him to be your lawful wedded husband, as long as you both shall live? Do you? ("I Do")

I, [Don Davis], take you, [Amy Owens], to be my (wife / husband), my best friend, and my soulmate.

When you need someone to encourage you, I want it to be me. When you need a helping hand, I want it to be mine. When you long for someone to smile at, turn to me. When you have something to share, share it with me.

I promise to give you my all and I know that I could not ask any different of you. Together, as one, we can accomplish anything.

This is my solemn vow to you.

Personalized Ring Vows

The Pastor will ask both the bride and the groom for the rings and make a brief comment about the importance and symbolism of the rings and then will come the vows with the exchanging of the rings. These are "repeat-after-me" vows. (The commas indicate pause)

I, Mark Clinton, take thee, Carmen Smith, to my wedded wife, to have and to hold, from this day forward, for richer for poorer, for better for worse, to be devoted unto thee, and to thee only, until the end of time. I pledge my heart, my body, and my soul to you. You are my strength, my shining light, my inspiration, and my passion. With this ring, I thee wed, with loyal love, I thee endow, all my worldly goods, with thee I share for all eternity.

I, Carmen Smith, take thee, Mark Clinton, to my wedded husband, to have and to hold, from this day forward, for richer for poorer, for better for worse, to be devoted unto thee, and to thee only, until the end of time. I pledge my heart, my body, and my soul to you. You are my strength, my shining light, my inspiration, and my passion. With this ring, I thee wed, with loyal love, I thee endow, all my worldly goods, with thee I share for all eternity.

I humbly give you my hand and my heart as a sanctuary of warmth and peace, and pledge my faith and love to you. Just as this circle is without end, my love for you is eternal. Just as it is made of incorruptible substance, my commitment to you will never fail. With this ring, I thee wed.

To marry the person you have set your heart upon is a joy unparalleled to human life. Angela, take this ring as a sign of my faith and commitment to our love, and share this joy with me today. Let it remind you always, as it circles your finger, of my eternal love, surrounding you and enfolding you day and night. With this ring, I seal the commitment I have made to you today; may you wear it proudly as my wife.

To marry the person you have set your heart upon is a joy unparalleled to human life. Stephen, take this ring as a sign of my faith and commitment to our love, and share this joy with me today. Let it remind you always, as it circles your finger, of my eternal love, surrounding you and enfolding you day and night. With this ring, I seal the commitment I have made to you today; may you wear it proudly as my husband.

I, Samuel Lemons, take thee, Mollie Baker, to my wedded wife, to have and to hold, for richer for poorer, for better for worse, as long as we both shall live. With this ring, I thee wed, in the name of the Father, and of the Son, and of the Holy Spirit, Amen.

I, Mollie Baker, take thee, Samuel Lemons, to my wedded husband, to have and to hold, for richer for poorer, for better for worse, as long as we both shall live. With this ring, I thee wed, in the name of the Father, and of the Son, and of the Holy Spirit, Amen.

(Samuel to Mollie) "Mollie, I give you this ring, as a symbol of my love and faithfulness. And take you as my wife, As it encircles your finger, may it remind you always, that you are surrounded, by my enduring love."

(Molly to Samuel) "Samuel, I give you this ring, as a symbol of my love and faithfulness. And take you as my husband, As it encircles your finger, may it remind you always, that you are surrounded, by my enduring love."

I, Carlos Bass, take thee, Audrey Kindle, to my wedded wife, to have and to hold, from this day forward, for richer for poorer, for better for worse, to be devoted unto thee, and to thee only, as long as we both shall live. With this ring, I thee wed, with loyal love, I thee endow, all my worldly goods, with thee I share my heart.

I, Audrey Kindle, take thee, Carlos Bass, to my wedded husband, to have and to hold, from this day forward, for richer for poorer, for better for worse, to be devoted unto thee, and to thee only, as long as we both shall live. With this ring, I thee wed, with loyal love, I thee endow , all my worldly goods, with thee I share my heart.

I, Peter take thee Heloise, to my wedded wife, to have and to hold, from this day forward, for richer for poorer, for better for worse, to be devoted unto thee, and to thee only, as long as we both shall live. With this ring, I thee wed, with loyal love, I thee endow, all my worldly goods, with thee I share,

You are as much a part of my being, as the beating of my own heart. When you hurt, I hurt. When you cry, I cry. When you rejoice, I rejoice. Where you go, I go. Wherever God leads us, I will be by your side. The one who created life, created us for each other, and because of his saving grace, not even death can part us. In the name of the Father, and of the Son, and of the Holy Spirit, Amen.

"I Heloise, take thee, Peter, to my wedded husband, to have and to hold, from this day forward, for richer for poorer, for better for worse, to be devoted unto thee, and to thee only, as long as we both shall live. With this ring, I thee wed, with loyal love, I thee endow. You are as much a part of my being , as the beating of my own heart. When you hurt, I hurt. When you cry, I cry. When you rejoice, I rejoice. Where you go, I go. Wherever God leads us, I will be by your side. The one who created life, created us for each other, And because of his saving grace, not even death can part us. In the name of the Father, and of the Son, and of the Holy Spirit, Amen.

I, Ronald, take you Julie to be my wife, my partner in life and my one true love. I will cherish our friendship and love you today, tomorrow, and forever. I will trust you and honor you. I will laugh with you and cry with you. I will love you faithfully through the best and the worst, through the difficult and the easy. What may come I will always be there. As I have given you my hand to hold, so I give you my life to keep. With this ring, I thee wed.

I, Julie, take you Ronald, to be my husband, my partner in life and my one true love. I will cherish our friendship and love you today, tomorrow, and forever. I will trust you and honor you. I will laugh with you and cry with you. I will love you faithfully through the best and the worst, through the difficult and the easy. What may come I will always be there. As I have given you my hand to hold, so I give you my life to keep. With this ring, I thee wed.

"I, Johnny Castle, give this ring as a sign of my love and faithfulness in the name of the Father, the Son and the Holy Spirit."

"I, June Dillon, give this ring as a sign of my love and faithfulness in the name of the Father, the Son and the Holy Spirit."

I, Thomas McNally, take thee Deborah Peters, to my wedded wife, to have and to hold, from this day forward, for richer for poorer, for better for worse., I give myself to you, and to only you, as long as we both shall live., With this ring, I thee wed, with loyal love, I thee endow, all my worldly goods, with thee I share, in the name of the Father, and of the Son, and of the Holy Spirit, Amen.

"I Deborah Peters, take thee, Thomas McNally, to my wedded husband, to have and to hold, from this day forward, for richer for poorer, for better for worse, I give myself to you, and to only you, as long as we both shall live. With this ring, I thee wed, with loyal love, I thee endow, in the name of the Father, and of the Son, and of the Holy Spirit, Amen.

I, Benson, take you, Angelique, to be my wife, my constant friend, my faithful partner and my love from this day forward. With this ring, in the presence of our family and friends, I give myself to you in marriage.

I, Angelique, take you, Benson, to be my husband, my constant friend, my faithful partner and my love from this day forward. With this ring, in the presence of our family and friends, I give myself to you in marriage.

I, Dominique Costello, take you, Michelle Adams to be my wedded wife. With this ring, I commit my life to our partnership in marriage. I promise to comfort you, to encourage you in all walks of life. I promise to express my thoughts and emotions to you and to listen to you in times of joy and in times of sorrow. I love you and you are my closest friend.

I, Michelle Adams, take you, Dominique Costello to be my wedded husband. With this ring, I commit my life to our partnership in marriage. I promise to comfort you, to encourage you in all walks of life. I promise to express my thoughts and emotions to you and to listen to you in times of joy and in times of sorrow. I love you and you are my closest friend.

[Don / Amy], I give you this ring as a symbol of our love. With it I wed you, and commit my life to you forever.

I, Mike, take you, Channing, to be my wife, my faithful partner in life, my best friend and my one true love. With this Ring, I promise to love you without reservation, in sickness and in health, for richer for poorer, to stand together in our times of joy and sorrow, always to be open and honest with you, for as long as we both shall live.

I, Channing, take you, Mike, to be my husband, my faithful partner in life, my best friend and my one true love. With this Ring, I promise to love you without reservation, in sickness and in health, for richer for poorer, to stand together in our times of joy and sorrow, always to be open and honest with you, for as long as we both shall live.

9. THE ORIGIN OF TRADITIONAL WEDDING VOWS

Section 1

The History of "The Original Wedding Ceremony"

Introduction

Perhaps you have heard the following phrases which have been used at wedding ceremonies of all kinds, both contemporary and traditional...

"Dearly beloved"
"holy matrimony"
"let him now speak or forever hold his peace"
"in prosperity and adversity"
"to have and to hold"
"for better for worse"
"for richer for poorer"
"in sickness and in health"
"to love and to cherish"
"till death us do part"

"wedded husband…wedded wife"
and,
"with this ring I thee wed"

These beautiful words have come to be a part of our expectation during a wedding ceremony. It seems that even in this modern and fast-paced day that when you attend a wedding, there is a comforting ring of familiarity to it. Something within us yearns for the reality of these inspiring words. Something about the tradition of the wedding ceremony and these simple phrases offer a sense of stability in an often unstable world.

Though so many versions exist and many couples now even choose to write their own vows, there are so many beloved phrases we continue to hear, want to hear and even expect to hear at a wedding. These phrases are so common and so widespread that there must be some common wedding ceremony from which they all spring. There must be some ancient ancestor which has given birth to the various ceremonies that we have today. And there is. "The Original Wedding Ceremony" in the English language dates back to the time of King Henry VIII and has much to do with the history of western civilization. Hang on for a quick trip back in time as we search for the author of "The Original Wedding Ceremony" in the English language.

The Connection to Rome and Latin

Rome ruled the world for a thousand years. Even after the Roman Empire crumbled around 400 AD, the language of Rome continued to rule Europe for another thousand years. People from England, France, Germany, Spain and England could all communicate through a common language, Latin. It was the language of commerce, politics, and, of course, religion. The Latin translation of the Bible, The Vulgate, translated by Jerome, was used by everyone. But people in different countries also spoke their own languages, French, Italian, Spanish, German, and English.

As more and more people spoke their native languages, fewer and fewer people spoke Latin. Although Latin was still the language of commerce, politics and religion, it was no longer the language of the common people. Only the educated and the influential spoke and read Latin. Church services, however, continued to be held in Latin by the Roman Catholic Church. This was destined to change since the church was begun for the common people to be led in a language that all could understand. In the middle of the second millennium there was a fresh wind blowing across Europe. A time of incredible change and innovation was peaking above the horizon.

The Link to Martin Luther and the Reformation

The Protestant Reformation began with Martin Luther in 1517. He challenged the practice of the church selling indulgences for sins. He tacked his 95 Theses to the door of Castle Church in Wittenberg, Germany on October 31, 1517. This was just 25 years after Columbus had discovered America. Martin Luther also translated the Bible into the German language.

The printing press, a true technological innovation that catapulted learning, communication, and civilization more radically than the computer, was invented in Germany only a few years earlier by Johannes Gutenberg. Martin Luther's German translation of the Bible was one of the first books ever printed. Luther translated the Bible into German to make it more accessible to the common people, a task he began alone in 1521 during his stay in the Wartburg Castle. He published the New Testament in September 1522. His translation reached the shores of England and had a profound effect on William Tyndale.

Tyndale translated the Bible into English. For his efforts of bringing the Bible into the language of the common people he was rewarded by being tried for heresy and treason and then strangled and burned at the stake. However, much of Tyndale's translation eventually found its way into the King James Version of the Bible published in 1611.What does any of this have to do with "The Original Wedding Ceremony?" Hang on for a couple more minutes. It gets more interesting.

The English Reformation

The Protestant Reformation led to a number of Christian churches in Europe breaking away from communion with the church in Rome. The English Reformation was part of a long running dispute with the Papacy concerning the jurisdiction it claimed over the English people. In the beginning, the English Reformation was more political that theological. This break with the Roman church took place during the reign of Henry VIII.

Henry VIII ascended to the throne of England in 1509 just before his 18th birthday. This was just eight years before Martin Luther posted his 95 Theses. Henry reigned from 1509 to 1547. During his reign, the church in England would be changed forever. He had been a devoted Catholic early in his reign. In fact, he had even defended the Papacy from Martin Luther's accusations of heresy in a book he wrote called "The Defense of the Seven Sacraments." He was awarded the title "Defender of the Faith" for his work by Pope Leo X. However, by the late 1520's Henry wanted to divorce his wife, Catherine of Aragon since she had not produced a male heir who survived into adulthood. Henry wanted more than anything else to have a male heir to succeed him. The Pope, however, refused to annul Henry's marriage to Catherine and Henry was not the type of man who would simply submit to a ruling like that from any source.

Henry called a Parliament in 1529 (12 years after the German Reformation and 8 years after the Bible was printed in German) to deal with the divorce, since the Pope refused to grant it. This Parliament lasted for seven years and passed many of the Acts which cut England's political ties to Rome. It has been called the Reformation Parliament. Though this English Reformation was more political than theological in the beginning, it produced sweeping theological changes. The monarch became the head of the English church and the Church of England was established. In a sense, England declared its independence from Rome.

The chief architect of the English Reformation was a man named Thomas Cranmer. Cranmer was born in 1489 (three years before Columbus sailed to America). He came to Henry's attention as a researcher who helped to compile legal and historical precedent for Henry's annulment from Catherine of Aragon. Cranmer traveled to Rome in 1530 and to Germany in 1532 on Henry's behalf. On March 30, 1533 after the death of William Warham, Thomas Cranmer was appointed Archbishop of Canterbury. In May he declared the marriage of Henry and Catherine void. Henry and Anne Boleyn were then legally married. In September of 1533 Anne gave birth to Henry's second daughter, Elizabeth, and Cranmer became her godfather.

Cranmer's reforms led to the formalization of the Church of England. With these reforms came the need for a new clergy and new services. The Catholic services in Latin needed to be replaced with worship services and rituals in English. King Henry VIII died in 1547 and his young son, Edward VI, son of Jane Seymore, Henry's third wife, became King. Edward was only a boy, but had been raised as a Protestant. Cranmer was an indispensable adviser to this boy King. In that same year, the requirements of the clergy to be celibate were lifted in England.

In 1549 Cranmer introduced the English Book of Common Prayer. This book was written to take the place of various Latin rituals which were in use in different parts of the country. This single volume in the English language could be used throughout England so that, "now from henceforth all the realm shall have but one use." Cranmer was responsible for the original 1549 version and its 1552 revision, The Book of Common Prayer

When it came to the wedding portion the book was revised again very slightly in 1559 under the reign of Queen Elizabeth and not again until 1662.

In writing the Book of Common Prayer, Archbishop Cranmer relied on a document that was in common use in

England within the Roman Catholic Church, The Use of York. The Roman Catholic church was very consistent in matters of judicial law, the sacraments and solemn fasts. The custom of the Roman Church had to be adhered to strictly. However, when it came to church services, each church was able to keep to its own traditions. So there came to be a number of local "Uses" or liturgical customs which came into accepted practice.

In England there were two primary "Uses," the Sarum Use, and The Use of York. The Sarum Use was used in the south and The Use of York was adhered to primarily in the north. The Use of York was related to York Minster. The Archbishop of York is the second highest position in the Anglican church today behind the Archbishop of Canterbury. There has been a Christian influence in York Minster since the 300's AD. Listen to the wording in The Use of York when it came to "troth-plighting," "Here I take thee N. to my wedded wife, to have and to hold at bed and at board, for fairer for fouler, for better for worse, in sickness and in health, till death us do part and thereto I plight thee my troth" Notice the absence of the words "if the holy church it will ordain," as in the Sarum Use and the English Catholic marriage ceremony.

King Edward died in 1553 and was succeeded by his sister, Mary. Mary was the daughter of Catherine of Aragon and loyal to the church of Rome. She set about to restore Roman Catholicism as the state church of England. Queen Mary had Archbishop Cranmer put into prison in 1554 and brought up on charges of heresy in 1556. He was sentenced to be burned at the stake and was executed on March 21, 1556. His story can be seen in Robert Bolt's "A Man for All Seasons."

The Shakespearean Quality of the Language

The question often asked is, "Why does 'The Original Wedding Ceremony' have such a Shakespearean quality to it?" The answer lies in the people who had such an awesome influence on the modern English language and the marriage ceremony. Most would agree that the three English works that had the most profound effect on the development of the modern English language are the King James Version of the Bible dating 1611, the works of William Shakespeare, and the Book of Common Prayer. Yet who were the men behind them?

William Shakespeare lived between 1564 and 1616 and wrote approximately 38 plays, 154 sonnets, and various other poems. He is widely regarded as the greatest writer of the English language and his plays have been translated into every major living language. His works enjoyed great popularity in his day and to the present day. He added a beauty to the language that went around the world through the expansion of the British Empire.

The King James Version of the Bible, or Authorized Version, was published in 1611, during the lifetime of Shakespeare. King James did not translate it, but merely authorized its translation into the English language. Henry VIII had previously authorized The Great Bible in 1540. The man who was primarily responsible for the language of the King James Bible, however, died 75 years earlier. William Tyndale (1494 – 1536) translated the Bible from the original Hebrew and Greek languages into English. Due to the relatively new invention of the printing press, his translation became widespread. Since it was illegal to have the Bible in the language of the common people, Tyndale was tried for heresy, strangled, and burned at the stake in Belgium with King Henry VIII's approval. Because of the high academic and literary quality of Tyndale's original translation most of it survived into the Authorized Version.

The Book of Common Prayer came as the result of the English Reformation. It was first written in 1549 (more than 450 years ago), just 13 years after William Tyndale's martyrdom. It was written by Thomas Cranmer, the Archbishop of Canterbury under Henry VIII and Edward VI. He revised it in 1552. Cranmer was also burned at the stake as a heretic by Queen Mary, the daughter of Henry VIII and the Spanish princess Catherine of Aragon. Mary's attempt to bring England back under Roman Catholicism was ultimately unsuccessful. Under Queen Elizabeth, who succeeded her half-sister Mary, the Book of Common Prayer was revised again slightly in 1559. This revision was used during the period of the greatest growth of the British Empire. It was the prayer book of William Shakespeare. The Book of Common Prayer (from which "The Original Wedding Ceremony" comes) was not revised again until 1662, and then only slightly. This version is still used today although it was updated in the 1960's. "The Original Wedding Ceremony" is actually a section of the Book of Common Prayer called, "The Form of Solemnization of Matrimony," which is included in Section 2 of this chapter.

The history of the English Bible and the English Book of Common Prayer are irrevocably intertwined into the history of England. William Tyndale died for his dedication to translating the Bible into the common language of the English people. Thomas Cranmer died for his convictions which are inscribed in the beautiful prose of the Book of Common Prayer. William Shakespeare popularized, expanded and beautified the language handed down to him. The ambitious British Empire, upon which the sun never set, launched the flowering English language of Tyndale, Cranmer, and Shakespeare around the world. It was the language of church, state, and entertainment for generations.

Some Ironies of "The Original Wedding Ceremony"

There are a few ironies which are associated with "The Original Wedding Ceremony." One irony is that King Henry VIII, who actively pushed for the separation of England and the Church of Rome, did so because he wanted a divorce which the Pope refused to grant. Thomas Cranmer, who he appointed Archbishop of Canterbury after the death of William Warham, did grant him a divorce and married him to his wife, Anne Boleyn, who was the mother of Elizabeth.

Another irony is that even though celibacy was the rule of the Catholic priesthood, the Protestant Reformation did not follow that rule, since it was non-biblical. Martin Luther, leader of the Reformation in Germany took a wife. Thomas Cranmer also took a wife while visiting in Germany and brought her back to England. Since the celibacy rules had not yet been changed in England, he had to keep her secretly.

Due to the re-organization of the church and state in England after the English Reformation, King Henry VIII became the official "Head of the Church." The irony of the situation is that he was married six times.

Another irony of "The Original Wedding Ceremony" has to do with its author. Thomas Cranmer, who wrote the Book of Common Prayer, was sentenced to be burned at the stake for heresy (because of his break with Roman Catholicism). When interrogated, he signed a statement recanting his theological views in order to avoid execution. It did him no good. According to John Foxe, Cranmer was allowed to make a public statement prior to his execution and he withdrew his recantation. He was tied by a chain to the stake and the fire was kindled and began to burn near him. He stretched out his right hand into the flames and held it there so that the people might see it burned since it was the hand that had signed his recantation. He repeatedly said, "this unworthy right hand!" Then, in the words of Stephen, the first Christian martyr, he said, "Lord Jesus, receive my spirit." The irony is that even though he had signed a recantation of his views with that right hand, he had also written the beautiful words of the Book of Common Prayer which are still in use today, including "The Original Wedding Ceremony." William Shakespeare was born 8 years after this event during the reign of Queen Elizabeth. Shakespeare used Thomas Cranmer as a supporting character in his play, "Henry VIII."

Conclusion

It was a time of monarchs and tremendous political, technological, and religious turmoil. There was little religious toleration in England which is the reason the Pilgrims sailed for America in 1620. The church and state were united, not separated, so there was no room for variation in the wedding ceremony as there is today. The British Empire spread around the globe during the reign of

Queen Elizabeth and so did the English Book of Common Prayer. In subsequent years the works of Shakespeare and the King James Version of the Bible also spread throughout the globe which accounts for the similarity of the language. The Church of England now uses a more modern book, Common Worship. The most recent royal weddings have used this ceremony. A more modern text with the name Book of Common Prayer is used in America in Episcopal and Methodist churches.

When we think of the elegance of "The Original Wedding Ceremony" and the eternal meaning that rings from its beloved phrases, we are all moved. It is the perfect marriage of beauty and truth. Who has not been stirred to tears either at their own wedding or someone else's by this meaningful ceremony. We do not know when exactly Thomas Cranmer first penned these words with that "right hand" of his, or if he borrowed some or all of them. We can only imagine what the first occasion of using this ceremony might have been, perhaps at the wedding of King Henry VIII and Anne Boleyn, or some unknown nobleman during the reign of King Edward. But one thing demands our attention. Before completely dismissing this ceremony and its prosaic wording as completely archaic and outdated, it is worthwhile to contemplate the profound and sacred meaning behind its prose, the seriousness of these vows, the multitudes who have lived by them, and the exceedingly great price that was paid by those who handed it down to us, imperfect as they were. The Book of Common Prayer is in the public domain in America.

Section 2

"The Original Wedding Ceremony"

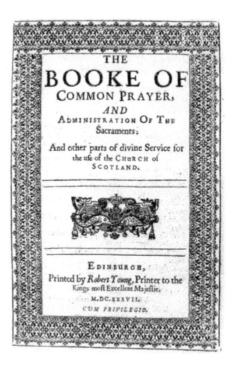

The following is taken from the Book of Common Prayer which is the official ministerial handbook of the Church of England. It is copied from a manuscript dating back to 1662 and the seeming spelling issues are due to the changes in the English language over the centuries.

The BOOK of
Common Prayer,
And Adminiſtration of the
SACRAMENTS,
AND OTHER

RITES and CEREMONIES
OF THE
CHURCH
According to the Ufe of
The CHURCH of ENGLAND:
TOGETHER WITH THE
PSALTER
OR
PSALMS of DAVID
Pointed as they are to be fung or faid in Churches
The Form of Solemnization of Matrimony

First the Banns of all that are to be married together must be published in the Church three several Sundays, during the time of Morning Service, or of Evening Service, (if there be no Morning Service,) immediately after the second Lesson; the Curate saying after the accustomed manner, I publish the Banns of Marriage between M. of ----- and N. of -----. If any of you know cause, or just impediment, why these two persons should not be joined together in holy Matrimony, ye are to declare it. This is the first [second, or third] time of asking.

And if the persons that are to be married dwell in divers Parishes, the Banns must be asked in both Parishes; and the Curate of the one Parish shall not solemnize Matrimony betwixt them, without a Certificate of the Banns being thrice asked, from the Curate of the other Parish.

At the day and time appointed for solemnization of Matrimony, the persons to be married shall come into the body of the Church with their friends and neighbours: and there standing together, the Man on the right hand, and the Woman on the left, the Priest shall say, DEARLY beloved, we are gathered together here in the sight of God, and in the face of this congregation, to join together this Man and this Woman in holy Matrimony; which is an honourable estate, instituted of God in the time of man's innocency, signifying unto us the mystical union that is betwixt Christ and his Church; which holy estate Christ adorned and beautified with his presence, and first miracle that he wrought, in Cana of Galilee; and is commended of Saint Paul to be honourable among all men: and therefore is not by any to be enterprised, nor taken in hand, unadvisedly, lightly, or wantonly, to satisfy men's carnal lusts and appetites, like brute beasts that have no understanding; but reverently, discreetly, advisedly, soberly, and in the fear of God; duly considering the causes for which Matrimony was ordained. First, It was ordained for the procreation of children, to be brought up in the fear and nurture of the Lord, and to the praise of his holy Name. Secondly, It was ordained for a remedy against sin, and to avoid fornication; that such persons as have not the gift of continency might marry, and keep themselves undefiled members of Christ's body. Thirdly, It was ordained for the mutual society, help, and comfort, that the one ought to have of the other, both in prosperity and adversity. Into which holy estate these two persons present come now to be joined. Therefore if any man can shew any just cause, why they may not lawfully be joined together, let him now speak, or else hereafter for ever hold his peace.

And also, speaking unto the persons that shall be married, he shall say,

I REQUIRE and charge you both, as ye will answer at the dreadful day of judgement when the secrets of all hearts shall be disclosed, that if either of you know any impediment, why ye may not be lawfully joined together in Matrimony, ye do now confess it. For be ye well assured, that so many as are coupled together otherwise than God's Word doth allow are not joined together by God; neither is their Matrimony lawful.

At which day of Marriage, if any man do allege and declare any impediment, why they may not be coupled together in Matrimony, by God's law, or the laws of this Realm; and will be bound, and sufficient sureties with him, to the parties; or else put in a caution (to the full value of such charges as the persons to be married do thereby sustain) to prove his allegation: then the solemnization must be deferred, until such time as the truth be tried.

If no impediment be alleged, then shall the Curate say unto the Man,

N. WILT thou have this woman to thy wedded wife, to live together after God's ordinance in the holy estate of Matrimony? Wilt thou love her, comfort her, honour, and keep her in sickness and in health; and, forsaking all other, keep thee only unto her, so long as ye both shall live?

The Man shall answer, I will.

Then shall the Priest say unto the Woman,

N. WILT thou have this man to thy wedded husband, to live together after God's ordinance in the holy estate of

Matrimony? Wilt thou obey him, and serve him, love, honour, and keep him in sickness and in health; and, forsaking all other, keep thee only unto him, so long as ye both shall live?

The Woman shall answer, I will.

Then shall the Minister say,

Who giveth this woman to be married to this man?

Then shall they give their troth to each other in this manner.

The Minister, receiving the Woman at her father's or friend's hands, shall cause the Man with his right hand to take the Woman by her right hand, and to say after him as followeth. I N. take thee N. to my wedded wife, to have and to hold from this day forward, for better for worse, for richer for poorer, in sickness and in health, to love and to cherish, till death us do part, according to God's holy ordinance; and thereto I plight thee my troth.

Then shall they loose their hands; and the Woman, with her right hand taking the Man by his right hand, shall likewise say after the Minister, I N. take thee N. to my wedded husband, to have and to hold from this day forward, for better for worse, for richer for poorer, in sickness and in health, to love, cherish, and to obey, till death us do part, according to God's holy ordinance; and thereto I give thee my troth.

Then shall they again loose their hands; and the Man shall give unto the Woman a Ring, laying the same upon the book with the accustomed duty to the Priest and Clerk. And the Priest, taking the Ring, shall deliver it unto the Man, to put it upon the fourth finger of the Woman's left hand. And the Man holding the Ring there, and taught by the Priest, shall say, WITH this ring I thee wed, with my body I thee worship, and with all my worldly goods I thee endow: In the Name of the Father, and of the Son, and of the Holy Ghost. Amen.

Then the Man leaving the Ring upon the fourth finger of the Woman's left hand, they shall both kneel down; and the Minister shall say,

Let us pray.

O ETERNAL God, Creator and Preserver of all mankind, Giver of all spiritual grace, the Author of everlasting life: Send thy blessing upon these thy servants, this man and this woman, whom we bless in thy Name; that, as Isaac and Rebecca lived faithfully together, so these persons may surely perform and keep the vow and covenant betwixt them made, (whereof this Ring given and received is a token and pledge,) and may ever remain in perfect love and peace together, and live according to thy laws; through Jesus Christ our Lord. Amen.

Then shall the Priest join their right hands together, and say,

Those whom God hath joined together let no man put asunder.

Then shall the Minister speak unto the people.

FORASMUCH as N. and N. have consented together in holy wedlock, and have witnessed the same before God and this company, and thereto have given and pledged their troth either to other, and have declared the same by giving and receiving of a Ring, and by joining of hands; I pronounce that they be Man and Wife together, In the Name of the Father, and of the Son, and of the Holy Ghost. Amen.

And the Minister shall add this Blessing.

GOD the Father, God the Son, God the Holy Ghost, bless, preserve, and keep you; the Lord mercifully with his favour look upon you; and so fill you with all spiritual benediction and grace, that ye may so live together in this life, that in the world to come ye may have life everlasting. Amen.

Then the Minister or Clerks, going to the Lord's Table, shall say or sing this Psalm following.

Beati omnes. Psalm 128.

BLESSED are all they that fear the Lord: and walk in his ways. For thou shalt eat the labour of thine hands: O well is thee, and happy shalt thou be. Thy wife shall be as the fruitful vine: upon the walls of thine house; Thy children like the olive-branches: round about thy table. Lo, thus shall the man be blessed: that feareth the Lord. The Lord from out of Sion shall so bless thee: that thou shalt see Jerusalem in prosperity all thy life long; Yea, that thou shalt see thy children's children: and peace upon Israel. Glory be to the Father, &c. As it was in the beginning, &c.

Or this Psalm.

Deus misereatur. Psalm 67.

GOD be merciful unto us, and bless us: and shew us the light of his countenance, and be merciful unto us. That thy way may be known upon earth: thy saving health among all nations. Let the people praise thee, O God: yea, let all the people praise thee. O let the nations rejoice and be glad: for thou shalt judge the folk righteously, and govern the nations upon earth. Let the people praise thee, O God: yea, let all the people praise thee. Then shall the earth bring forth her increase: and God, even our own God, shall give us his blessing. God shall bless us: and all the ends of the world shall fear him. Glory be to the Father, &c. As it was in the beginning, &c.

The Psalm ended, and the Man and the Woman kneeling before the Lord's Table, the Priest standing at the Table, and turning his face towards them, shall say, Lord, have mercy upon us. Answer. Christ, have mercy upon us. Minister. Lord, have mercy upon us.

OUR Father, which art in heaven, Hallowed be thy Name. Thy kingdom come. Thy will be done in earth, as it is in heaven. Give us this day our daily bread. And forgive us our trespasses, As we forgive them that trespass against us. And lead us not into temptation; But deliver us from evil. Amen.

Minister. O Lord, save thy servant, and thy handmaid; Answer. Who put their trust in thee. Minister. O Lord, send them help from thy holy place; Answer. And evermore defend them. Minister. Be unto them a tower of strength,

Answer. From the face of their enemy. Minister. O Lord, hear our prayer. Answer. And let our cry come unto thee.

Minister.

O GOD of Abraham, God of Isaac, God of Jacob, bless these thy servants, and sow the seed of eternal life in their hearts; that whatsoever in thy holy Word they shall profitably learn, they may in deed fulfil the same. Look, O Lord, mercifully upon them from heaven, and bless them. And as thou didst send thy blessing upon Abraham and Sarah, to their great comfort, so vouchsafe to send thy blessing upon these thy servants; that they obeying thy Will, and alway being in safety under thy protection, may abide in thy love unto their lives' end; through Jesus Christ our Lord. Amen.

This Prayer next following shall be omitted, where the Woman is past child-bearing.

O MERCIFUL Lord, and heavenly Father, by whose gracious gift mankind is increased: We beseech thee, assist with thy blessing these two persons, that they may both be fruitful in procreation of children, and also live together so long in godly love and honesty, that they may see their children Christianly and virtuously brought up, to thy praise and honour; through Jesus Christ our Lord. Amen.

O GOD, who by thy mighty power hast made all things of nothing; who also (after other things set in order) didst appoint, that out of man (created after thine own image and similitude) woman should take her beginning; and, knitting them together, didst teach that it should never be lawful to put asunder those whom thou by Matrimony hadst made one: O God, who hast consecrated the state of Matrimony to such an excellent mystery, that in it is signified and represented the spiritual marriage and unity betwixt Christ and his Church: Look mercifully upon these thy servants, that both this man may love his wife, according to thy Word, (as Christ did love his spouse the Church, who gave himself for it, loving and cherishing it even as his own flesh,) and also that this woman may be loving and amiable, faithful and obedient to her husband; and in all quietness, sobriety, and peace, be a follower of holy and godly matrons. O Lord, bless them both, and grant them to inherit thy everlasting kingdom; through Jesus Christ our Lord. Amen.

Then shall the Priest say,

ALMIGHTY God, who at the beginning did create our first parents, Adam and Eve, and did sanctify and join them together in marriage; Pour upon you the riches of his grace, sanctify and bless you, that ye may please him both in body and soul, and live together in holy love unto your lives' end. Amen.

After which, if there be no Sermon detailing the duties of Man and Wife, the Minister shall read as followeth.

ALL ye that are married, or that intend to take the holy estate of Matrimony upon you, hear what the holy Scripture doth say as touching the duty of husbands towards their wives, and wives towards their husbands. Saint Paul, in his Epistle to the Ephesians, the fifth Chapter, doth give this commandment to all married men; Husbands, love your wives, even as Christ also loved the Church, and gave himself for it, that he might sanctify and cleanse it with the washing of water, by the Word; that he might present it to himself a glorious Church, not having spot, or wrinkle, or any such thing; but that it should be holy, and without blemish. So ought men to love their wives as their own bodies. He that loveth his wife loveth himself: for no man ever yet hated his own flesh, but nourisheth and cherisheth it, even as the Lord the Church: for we are members of his body, of his flesh, and of his bones. For this cause shall a man leave his father and mother, and shall be joined unto his wife; and they two shall be one flesh. This is a great mystery; but I speak concerning Christ and the Church. Nevertheless, let every one of you in particular so love his wife, even as himself. Likewise the same Saint Paul, writing to the Colossians, speaketh thus to all men that are married; Husbands, love your wives, and be not bitter against them. Hear also what Saint Peter, the Apostle of Christ, who was himself a married man, saith unto them that are married; Ye husbands, dwell with your wives according to knowledge; giving honour unto the wife, as unto the weaker vessel, and as being heirs together of the grace of life, that your prayers be not hindered. Hitherto ye have heard the duty of the husband toward the wife. Now likewise, ye wives, hear and learn your duties toward your husbands, even as it is plainly set forth in holy Scripture. Saint Paul, in the aforenamed Epistle to the Ephesians, teacheth you thus; Wives, submit yourselves unto your own husbands, as unto the Lord. For the husband is the head of the wife, even as Christ is the head of the Church: and he is the Saviour of the body. Therefore as the Church is subject unto Christ, so let the wives be to their own husbands in every thing. And again he saith, Let the wife see that she reverence her husband. And in his Epistle to the Colossians, Saint Paul giveth you this short lesson; Wives, submit yourselves unto your own husbands, as it is fit in the Lord. Saint Peter also doth instruct you very well, thus saying; Ye wives, be in subjection to your own husbands; that, if any obey not the Word, they also may without the Word be won by the conversation of the wives; while they behold your chaste conversation coupled with fear. Whose adorning, let it not be that outward adorning of plaiting the hair, and of wearing of gold, or of putting on of apparel; but let it be the hidden man of the heart, in that which is not corruptible; even the ornament of a meek and quiet spirit, which is in the sight of God of great price. For after this manner in the old time the holy women also, who trusted in God, adorned themselves, being in subjection unto their own husbands; even as Sarah obeyed Abraham, calling him lord; whose daughters ye are as long as ye do well, and are not afraid with any amazement.

It is convenient that the new-married persons should receive the holy Communion at the time of their Marriage, or at the first opportunity after their Marriage.

The Form of Solemnization of Matrimony

(taken from the Book of Common Prayer, 1662 revision)

Conclusion

It is quite evident that the many of the rich and beautiful phrases that are so pregnant with meaning have been used in wedding ceremonies in the English language for 500 years. Many of them were translated from the Latin wedding ceremonies. When considering the depth of meaning and the heritage of this beautiful ceremony and these time tested vows, it is certainly worth the consideration of the modern couple that these vows are in still in use for a reason. They are meaningful. Their meaning is understood by all. The couple who uses them is standing in line with so many of the great men and women of the English speaking world, including kings and queens, cooks and waitresses, princes and princesses, and an uncountable throng. While uniqueness is a good thing, there are a few occasions which unite our culture that call for a more traditional, meaningful, consistent approach.

10. SEVEN CREATIVE WRITING TIPS

Since writing your own wedding vows is a creative process and cannot necessarily be done in 10 minutes before the ceremony (you will have other things on your mind then anyway), it will help to have a few ideas of how to help the creative process along. Not everyone is a writer. Not everyone has the creative "gene." Not everyone can sit down at a table for 30 minutes or an hour at a time and write. Since we realize that writing is a creative process and our brains need time to process information, and methods, and organization, we are going to give you just a few simple ideas that may help you "get the ball rolling" in your own writing process.

You need a place to write down your thoughts and ideas "as you have them." You will be surprised at how your mind will suddenly have a thought or an idea about what you want to include in your wedding vows or how you want to word those vows when you least expect it. Your brain is an amazing creative computer that never really stops. It continues to work on a problem even when you are busy doing other important things. It even works while you are asleep. God really has blessed you with an incredible tool.

So, how do we take advantage of the creative aspect of this tool? Well, here is a general rule: When your brain gives you an idea, write it down immediately. You might think that if your brain is so amazing, then why can't I just remember it and write it down later? Maybe you can, but that is only if you are able to find the file where you left it. For example, have you ever written a document on your computer and then for some reason you had to leave it or close it quickly and when you went back to retrieve it, you could not find it? Perhaps it was filed in an unusual folder, or even on a different drive. It can be very frustrating when you know that you wrote it and then you cannot retrieve it when needed. That is why it is so important when you have an inspired or creative thought to "write it down immediately."

Someone said that the weakest ink is better than the strongest memory. Great writers and speakers have usually developed some kind of system for writing down their thoughts when they have them. I personally have a journal of thoughts and ideas that I want to develop in the future. You may have a journal like this, too, in your mind, somewhere, that you have never written down. By the way, you can use these methods any time that you need to be creative.

Here are a few practical tips for recording some of the words or phrases or ideas that will come to your mind.

1st Tip
Write in this book.

Many people are afraid to write in a book. They remember their parents or teachers told them not to write in their books. However, in college, you really needed to take notes and highlight ideas in your text books. In fact, when I bought used text books, I actually looked for some that had already been highlighted and where someone had jotted notes in the margins. Their notes helped me study. Even though your parents and teachers told you not to write or scribble in your books, there were a few books that they told you it was OK to write in such as coloring books and puzzle books. They were going to be your books to keep and they were for the purpose of writing in. Think of this book (and many other topical books) as being your very own coloring book, puzzle book, or text book that you are free to write in, highlight, scribble in, doodle, or whatever you want. We have even provided spaces just for that purpose. You might even be able to write your entire wedding vows right on these pages. It is your wedding vow workbook.

There are places provided throughout this book where you may write personal thoughts, ideas, phrases, to remember for later. In chapter 2, you will find 10 tips for writing your own wedding vows. There is a space provided after each of these tips where you can write a few lines if you want to. There is also a space at the end of that chapter. Most of the chapters have a space at the end where you can take notes. Chapters 4 and 8 have actual wedding vows. Those are good places to highlight, underline, or circle key words or phrases. Chapters 5 and 6 are filled with romantic quotes about love and marriage. Those chapters are also great places to highlight, underline, or circle key phrases. There is also much margin space for writing your own thoughts. And, of course, the same goes for the list of romantic words in chapter 7.

This is your own personal workbook. Write your name in it and your contact information in case you lose it and someone needs to get it back to you. Hang onto it. In fact, in years to come, when you think about your wedding and the words you said to each other, you may just want to come back and read through this again and remember some of the thoughts you had. For that reason, it will be a good idea to take a copy of the actual vows that you do use and staple them into the back of this book. Who knows, your children might enjoy reading them someday.

2nd Tip
Keep some 3 x 5 cards with you.

Many great speakers and writers have maintained the habit for years of keeping a few 3 x 5 cards in their pocket or purse. You never know when a moment of inspiration will come upon you. You never know when you will hear a story, or see something that will spark your creative juices. Having a pen and your note cards will allow you to capture those thoughts and remember them. Some people prefer a small spiral notepad in place of note cards. Use whatever you will actually carry with you and use.

3rd Tip
Use your smart phone as a note card.

Some of the smart phones, like the iPhone, have a notepad that you can use to take notes. I use mine for grocery lists, addresses, words from songs, almost any random thing I need to remember. They can be easily erased when I no longer need the information. I also use it to write down ideas for things I want to write, or ideas I want to pursue. Sometimes I just need a place to write them down quickly until I can record them to my journal or computer. The notepad on my phone gives me the ability to do this quickly and easily and I always have my phone with me. Many people today carry their tablet with them everywhere. Use whatever device will work.

4th Tip
Use a digital voice recorder.

Some people prefer to say the words instead of writing the words. They speak and hear better than they write. Perhaps you have heard someone say they were just "thinking out loud." A lot of people really do "think out loud." If you are one of those people, then try carrying a digital voice recorder. You can find some that are very inexpensive. You may even have one on your phone, or if not, you may find an ap for it that you can put on your phone. Say what you are thinking. Say it several ways. Then write it down later. Yes, you will still need to write it down, but at least your creative juices will not be stifled by the writing process since you will only have to say the words into the recorder. Writing them will just be transcribing what you said. And, of course, you can use the writing process to edit what you have said.

5th Tip
Use a white board.

Most people are visual. They think visually and remember visually. For this reason, a white board is an excellent tool to help us think, create, and remember. If you remember back to your school days, what did your teacher use to help you learn? Where were your assignments usually written? How did he or she show you how to work out the problems? It was on the white board.

Get a small white board that you can dedicate to the process of writing your own wedding vows. Keep it in your room or wherever you will see it every day. Write down the phrases you have been thinking of. What a great place to write and edit things instantly! Having it visually in front of you will keep it on your mind, too, until you have decided exactly what you want to say. In fact, using a white board may be the best tool you have for editing what you have written.

6th Tip
Create a Word document.

Early in the process of writing your own vows you will need to create a Word document, or whatever kind of software you prefer. I like notepad because it is so quick and simple to use. I mentioned Word because it also has a synonym feature. You can actually right click on the word you want to improve and find a similar word that might be more descriptive. Transfer your thoughts and ideas from your note cards or smart phone or this book into your Word document on your computer and you can edit there and keep a soft copy of your wedding vows. You can print it out when you are ready. You can also email it to a friend who you want to proof read it for you. You will probably also need to send a copy to your minister for him or her to proofread and approve.

7th Tip
Sleep on it.

I like this one. After you have written out your vows edited them and printed them out. Sleep on it for a day or two. It may be that you will have a revelation. Something that you thought was brilliant or clever or witty when you said it or wrote it, you might have second thoughts about. Take those second thoughts seriously. Keep in mind what your love will think when she hears them. Will she or he be embarrassed or upset by what you have said? Will the crowd understand your reference or inside joke? If not, then you may want to reconsider it. If you have a question, then ask a close friend, someone who will be honest with you, for their opinion. You may also ask your wedding officiant for his or her opinion or advice.

Conclusion

Using a few of these tips should help you to write the perfect vows. Like anything else in life, you will get out of it what you put into the process. One specific word of caution is to avoid procrastination. Procrastination can be a killer in any endeavor, especially when it comes to writing. Take some time to let your thoughts ripen and ferment. The good news is that there are many helpful things in these pages that will help to speed up the process.

11. THE 30 MINUTE WEDDING VOW TEMPLATE

This template is designed for those who simply must have their wedding vows in a short period of time and are at a loss for how to put their feelings into words. Work through this wedding vow template and choose the words that best express how you feel. There is a set order to follow There are 4 statements with a place provided to write you own unique thoughts using one or more of the "Ten Tips" provided in Chapter 2. A combination of those tips is provided in italics as an example.

There are certain places where you can choose the words that best suit you or your spouse. You may also opt to drop the phrase or phrases that are supplied completely and insert your own phrase. This template gives you a specific order to follow and specific suggestions for wording, but still allows you the creativity to add or substitute words or phrases that only you would think of to say to your love.

Feel free to use this template it in an "emergency" or just as a way of getting you started. The words or phrases inside the parentheses are suggested choices and are based on the timeless beauty and meaningful concepts of the classic wedding vows. You may also choose to insert your own words instead of the words that are supplied. The simplest way may be to underline the phrases you want to use and then rewrite them in this book, or on a separate sheet of paper.

Statement 1

[Fiancé(e)'s first name], you are, (the love of my life, the best thing that ever happened to me, my sun moon and stars, the light of my life, the one I love with all of my being, light up my life with your unselfish love). And I cannot (imagine, dream of, think of) (a life, living a life, enduring life, what the rest of my life would be, picture any version of my life) without you.

————————•●●●•————————

_____

_____

_____

_____

_____

_____

_____

Insert One or More of the "Ten Tips" Next

This would be a good place to make the vows more customized by using one of the "Ten Tips" that are mentioned in Chapter 2. You can use one or two of those ten tips to tailor your wedding vows to your fiancé(e). The following statement in italics is an example of how to mix 2 or 3 of those tips into one statement.

I will never forget the very first time I saw you and was captivated by your big brown eyes and radiant smile. And I am still captivated by every glance, and always will be. I love you for your warm and tender heart, and your strong and steady character. I eagerly look forward to being your helper, encourager, lover and best friend.

————————— •●●• —————————

_____

_____

_____

_____

_____

_____

_____

_____

Statement 2

Standing here with you today (in the presence of God and all these people, in the presence of God and our friends and family, publicly), is (the greatest moment of my life, a dream come true, a fairy tale in real life, my greatest achievement, the happiest moment of my life, the thrill of my life, the proudest moment of my life, makes me so grateful to God).

———————•●●●•———————

———————————————————————

———————————————————————

———————————————————————

———————————————————————

———————————————————————

———————————————————————

———————————————————————

———————————————————————

———————————————————————

———————————————————————

———————————————————————

———————————————————————

Statement 3

Today, in this place, (before God and all these present, in the presence of God and these witnesses, in the presence of God and our peers), I promise (with all of my heart, with all of my heart and soul, with everything that is in me, with every fiber of my being) to love you (in the good times and bad times, in the happy times and sad times, when you are healthy or when you are ill), to cherish you (when I feel like it and when I do not feel like it, no matter what life tosses our way), to honor you (before God and others, before all people, before friends and family, as God's precious gift to me), to be (true, true and faithful, faithfully devoted, faithful, true and loyal, totally devoted) to you (and you alone, and you only, forsaking all others), (as long as I live, as long as God gives me breath, as long as I can draw a breath, until I draw life's last breath, until my heart no longer beats, until the last beat of my heart, until the final beat of my mortal heart).

―――――――――•●●•―――――――――

_____

_____

_____

_____

_____

_____

Statement 4

(Now, Right now, Today, Today and Forevermore) I take you, [insert Name], (as my lawful husband, as my lawful wife, as my husband, as my wife, to be my lawful husband, to be my lawful wife) (for as long as we live, until death do us part, until we are parted in death, until only death can separate us, for the rest of my life, until we are parted by death, all the days of my life).

―――――――••••••―――――――

Personal Notes

THANK YOU

Thanks so much for taking the time to purchase this Kindle eBook, or paperback version of "How To Write Wedding Vows: A Wedding Vow Workbook." I sincerely hope it has been a blessing to you and helped you write the beautiful and memorable vows that you will treasure for a lifetime. If you enjoyed it, **please take a moment to leave a positive review at Amazon** so others will be aware of this resource. Also, check out a couple of my other Kindle eBooks or paperbacks at Amazon.com.

Kindest Regards,

Dr. Kelly Carr

ABOUT THE AUTHOR

Dr. Carr is an ordained minister and has been performing weddings for over 25 years. He holds degrees in ministry from Liberty University, Dallas Theological Seminary, and Southwestern Baptist Theological Seminary. He has been involved in church ministry as a Pastor and Youth Pastor, Minster of Education, and Church Planter for more than 25 years, also holding leadership positions in his denomination at the local, state, and national levels. He has performed more than 500 weddings and wedding renewals. Dr. Carr truly enjoys helping young couples prepare for their weddings and their new life together.

He believes that marriage is more than a beautiful ceremony. It is two lives joined in joyous partnership with common goals and values. Good relationships require work and a good start is always a benefit. He pastors in Greenville, Texas and lives with his beautiful wife his three awesome children. He still enjoys performing weddings in Greenville, McKinney, Rockwall, and the surrounding area.

He has also written A Guidebook for Searchers: Evidence Behind Our Faith; and Revelation: Book of Mystery and Majesty. His e-books include, The Wedding Vow Kit ebook, The Wedding Rehearsal Genie; The Wedding Income Toolkit for Ministers and Officiates; and The Daily Prayer Journal.

His websites include…
www.WeddingVowKit.com
www.WeddingIncome.com
www.ArizonaWeddingsPastor.com
www.HigherPurposeMinistries.com

WRITE YOUR VOWS HERE

_____

_____

_____

_____

_____

_____

_____

_____

_____

_____

_____

_____

_____

_____

_____

_____

_____

SOURCES CONSULTED

Anastasio, Janet and Michelle Bevilacqua. The Everything Wedding Vows Book. Holbrook, Massachusetts: Adams Media Corporation, 1994.

Chapman, Morris H. The Wedding Collection. Nashville: Broadman Press, 1991.

Criswell, W. A. Criswell's Guidebook for Pastors. Nashville: Broadman Press, 1980.

Fried, Katrina, and Lena Tabori. The Little Big Book for Brides. New York: Welcome Books, 2003.

Munro, Eleanor. Wedding Readings: Centuries of Writing and Rituals for Love and Marriage. New York: Viking, 1989.

Roney, Carley. The Knot's Complete Guide to Weddings in the Real World. New York: Broadway Books, 1998.

Warner, Diane. Complete Book of Wedding Toasts. Franklin Lakes, New Jersey: Career Press, 1997.

Warner, Diane. Complete Book of Wedding Vows. Franklin Lakes, New Jersey: Career Press, 1996.

CONTACT INFORMATION

This is a very important book. If you happen to find this book, please contact us at the information below so we can make plans to retrieve it. Thank you so much.

Name: _____

Phone: _____

Email: _____

Other: _____

_____

_____

Printed in Great Britain
by Amazon

45862850R00079